Let's Learn About MATTER

HARDNESS

Rebecca Kraft Rector

Enslow Publishing
101 W. 23rd Street
Suite 240
New York, NY 10011
USA

enslow.com

WORDS TO KNOW

atom A tiny bit of matter.

chemical Having to do with chemistry.

chemistry The science that deals with the properties of matter and how it forms and changes.

dent A dip or hole in a material.

gas A kind of matter that has no permanent shape, like air.

liquid A kind of matter that can move freely, like water.

physical Having to do with being able to be touched or seen.

properties The qualities or features of something.

solid A kind of matter that is firm and keeps its shape.

Contents

**Matter is everywhere.
Some of it is hard,
and some of it is soft.**

What Is Matter?

Matter is everything around you. All things are made of matter. Tiny bits of matter are called atoms. Atoms join together to make molecules.

FAST FACT

Even people are made of matter.

Cookies are solid, hot chocolate is a liquid, and steam is a gas.

Common Forms of Matter

Matter has different forms. Matter can be solid. A car is a solid. Matter can be liquid. Milk is a liquid. Matter can be a gas. Air is a mix of gases.

Fast Fact

Atoms are packed tightly together in a solid.

Food goes through a chemical change when you eat it. It also has physical properties like color, size, and shape.

Properties of Matter

Properties tell about matter. Physical properties tell how it acts, looks, and feels. Is it big or small? Hard or soft? Chemical properties let matter change. An example is how easily something explodes.

**This pyramid in Egypt is made of stone.
It has lasted for thousands of years.**

The Property of Hardness

Hardness is a physical property. It is a property of solid matter. Hard matter is firm. It is strong. It does not change shape easily. It is not easy to break.

FAST FACT

Hard materials are good for building.

This scale shows how hard different minerals are. It also shows the hardness of some common objects.

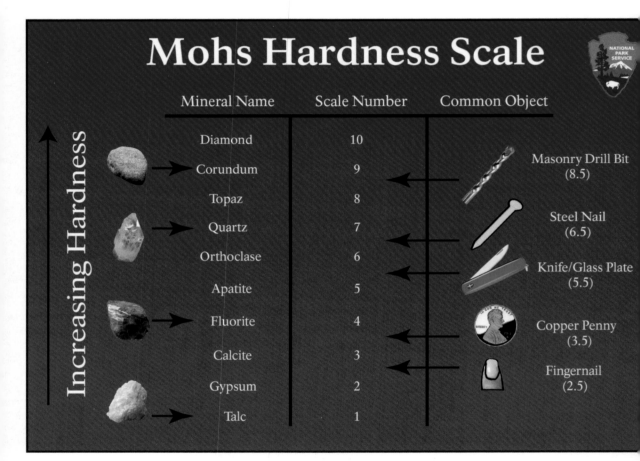

Mohs Hardness Scale

Mineral Name	Scale Number	Common Object
Diamond	10	
Corundum	9	Masonry Drill Bit (8.5)
Topaz	8	
Quartz	7	Steel Nail (6.5)
Orthoclase	6	Knife/Glass Plate (5.5)
Apatite	5	
Fluorite	4	Copper Penny (3.5)
Calcite	3	Fingernail (2.5)
Gypsum	2	
Talc	1	

Increasing Hardness

Can You Scratch It?

Hardness tells how easy it is to scratch materials. It is not easy to scratch diamonds. Diamonds are very hard. It is easy to scratch bananas. Bananas are soft.

FAST FACT

Use a fingernail, a coin, or a screw to scratch for hardness.

If a bicycle
tire is soft,
you can push
it in easily. If it
is full of air, it
will be hard to
make a dent.

Can You Dent It?

Try another test for hardness. Push on concrete. You cannot make a dent. It is hard. Push a pillow. You can make a dent. It is soft.

Squeeze a rock. You cannot change its shape. It is too hard.

Use Your Senses

Feel and listen for hardness. Squeeze a marshmallow. Is it squishy? Hard things aren't squishy. Tap on it. Does it make a noise? Hard things make a noise.

FAST FACT

Bells must be hard to make a sound. A soft bell will not ring.

These frozen berries are hard. They will become soft when they thaw.

Hard to Soft

Some things change from hard to soft. Hard candles melt. They become soft wax. Hard apples ripen. They become soft. Cooked apples are even softer.

Bread goes from soft to hard when it is toasted.

Soft to Hard

Some things change from soft to hard. Bread is soft. Toasted bread is hard. Clay is soft. Put it in an oven. Now it is hard.

FAST FACT

Turtle shells are soft at birth.

Activity

Scratch It!

Which is harder?
Let's get started!

Procedure:

Step 1: Straighten the
paper clip.

Step 2: Scratch a rock with your
fingernail.

Step 3: Is there a scratch on the rock?
The rock is softer than your
fingernail.

Step 4: If there was no change, scratch

the same rock with the end of the paper clip.

Step 5: Is there a scratch on the rock? The rock is softer than the paperclip. No change? The rock is harder than the paper clip.

Step 6: Repeat the test with more rocks.

You can scratch rocks to test for hardness

Learn More

Books

Masterson, Josephine. *Hard and Soft.* New York, NY: Rosen Publishing, 2016.

Minden, Cecilia. *Hard and Soft*. Ann Arbor, MI: Cherry Lake Publishing, 2016.

Rompella, Natalie. *Experiments in Material and Matter with Toys and Everyday Stuff.* North Mankato, MN: Capstone, 2016.

Websites

BBC
www.bbc.co.uk / schools / scienceclips / ages / 7_8 / rocks_soils.shtml
Test the hardness of different materials with this fun game.

BBC Bitesize
www.bbc.com / bitesize / guides / zgb9kqt / revision / 1
Find out why some materials are harder than others.

Index

Published in 2020 by Enslow Publishing, LLC.
101 W. 23rd Street, Suite 240, New York, NY 10011

Copyright © 2020 by Enslow Publishing, LLC.

All rights reserved.

No part of this book may be reproduced by any means without the written permission of the publisher.

Library of Congress Cataloging-in-Publication Data

Names: Rector, Rebecca Kraft, author.
Title: Hardness / Rebecca Kraft Rector.
Description: New York : Enslow Publishing, [2020] | Series: Let's learn about matter | Includes bibliographical references and index. | Audience: K to grade 4.
Identifiers: LCCN 2018048400 | ISBN 9781978507562 (library bound) | ISBN 9781978509108 (pbk.) | ISBN 9781978509115 (6 pack)
Subjects: LCSH: Matter—Properties—Juvenile literature. | Hardness—Juvenile literature.
Classification: LCC QC173.36 .R428 2020 | DDC 530.4—dc23

LC record available at https://lccn.loc.gov/2018048400

Printed in the United States of America

To Our Readers: We have done our best to make sure all website addresses in this book were active and appropriate when we went to press. However, the author and the publisher have no control over and assume no liability for the material available on those websites or on any websites they may link to. Any comments or suggestions can be sent by e-mail to customerservice@enslow.com.

Photos Credits: Cover, pp. 1, 16 T-gomo/Shutterstock.com; p. 4 Jose Luis Pelaez/Photographer's Choice/Getty Images; p. 6 © iStockphoto.com/Ivan Bajic; p. 8 Zoriana Zaitseva/Shutterstock.com; p. 10 Alfredo Garcia Saz/Shutterstock.com; p. 12 National Park Service; p. 14 greenphotoKK/Shutterstock.com; p. 18 Shebeko/Shutterstock.com; p. 20 Chones/Shutterstock.com; p. 23 Smit/Shutterstock.com; interior design elements (rock) chittakorn59/Shutterstock.com, (molecules) 123dartist/Shutterstock.com.